Traffic Jam
© Jennifer Bogush
Trade Edition, 2015
ISBN 978-1-63092-073-9

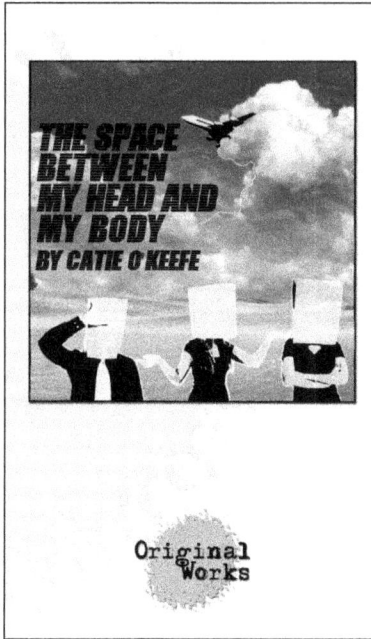

The Space Between My Head And My Body
By Catie O'Keefe

Synopsis: Thousands of feet above the earth minds and boundaries are becoming blurred. The plane seems to be in trouble and the flight attendant is off duty - but its all okay, because Dolly's packed an emergency kit and knitted this lovely life jacket. A darkly comic exploration of the strain it can take to force a mind and body to fit.

Cast Size: 2 Males, 2 Females (playing multiple roles)

Traffic Jam

**A play in one act
By Jennifer Bogush**

TRAFFIC JAM was originally produced at THE NEW YORK INTERNATIONAL FRINGE FESTIVAL, a production of THE PRESENT COMPANY.

The Original Cast was as follows:

Cassie—Jennifer Bogush
Gary—Jeff Branson
Death—Joe Tuttle

The action takes place in a hospital waiting room.

Time: The Present

Set Requirements: A few chairs.

Props: A scythe, soda cans, small alcohol bottles, a large purse, and magazines.

TRAFFIC JAM

SCENE 1: TRAFFIC JAM

(It is late afternoon in a hospital waiting room. Cassie, a train wreck, sits facing out. Near her, with his back to the audience, is her Brother.)

CASSIE: I'm not moving from this chair. And, I don't want to talk about it anymore. I don't know what you want me to say, you really want me to go in there and tell him, what, I love him? I don't know what that means. Let me get this straight, he's dying, so he gets off with a cancer pass, right? Everything's erased. Right? Not my problem. And, I'm not gonna go in there and spout this love shit for Mom's sake either, because I don't even think it's love she feels for him. Yeah, we have the same blood. Um, is that supposed to make me feel good? Because it makes me want to rip my eyeballs out! I can't sleep at night because of it. So, do you know what I do? I imagine cancer as little Ms. PacMans. Little Ms. PacMans with pink bows happily munching away at his flesh. I know. I'm super evil because it gives me piece of mind to know that he's on the table in there rotting from the inside out. I love that. I fucking love that! And, if I have to hear the myth of the drowning one more time, I'm gonna puke. How he pulled me out of the water! I don't remember it, so it didn't happen.

And, even if it did happen, it wasn't me dying he was scared of, it was how the shit would have interfered with his life. Well, now this shit is interfering with my life. This is unbelievable. You just want me to keep the hamster wheel going. Right? To be a whore, basically. You want my body to go in there and mouth words I don't believe in. Right? Right. I am not moving from this chair.

(He exits as Gary, a handsome young man, enters a moment later, sits down and closes his eyes. Cassie bounces her leg in the air and chomps on her gum. After a moment, she taps the arm of the chair with her fingernails. Gary shoots her piercing glances, which she doesn't seem to see.)

CASSIE: I have a boyfriend.

GARY: Excuse me?

CASSIE: I see you staring at me, and I thought it would be kinder to inform you that I have a boyfriend. Before you make an ass of yourself.

(He stares at her.)

CASSIE: I don't know sign language, but I could draw you a diagram if you're slow. Or, I could kick you in the balls if that would help clarify things for you.

GARY: You were tapping.

CASSIE: Yeah, well, I'm bored. Humans weren't made to wait this long. Monkeys maybe. Fucking chimps with bananas. Guess I'm a chimp today. You, too. Tuesday is chimp day. Did you get the memo?

GARY: So, you either tap or talk. Is there a third choice?

CASSIE: Besides, what was staring gonna do?

GARY: Honestly?

CASSIE: No, let's skip to the end of our relationship, and you can lie to me. Like everyone else in my life.

GARY: I was "willing" you to stop tapping.

CASSIE: "Willing" me.

GARY: Yes.

CASSIE: Um, yeah, you're on the wrong floor. If you take a left, you can take the elevator up to six. I believe the crazies reside there.

GARY: Laugh away, but it works.

CASSIE: ... When?

GARY: What?

CASSIE: When does it work?

GARY: At the movies. No one ever sits in front of me. If I see anyone coming, I give them the "Death Stare."

CASSIE: This works.

GARY: Absolutely.

CASSIE: And, today?

GARY: The equipment must be defective. I'll have to send it out for repair.

CASSIE: Try it on that lady.

GARY: Which?

CASSIE: Over there! That babbling nurse.

(He tries.)

GARY: Nope. Not working. Definitely broken. Besides, what if she's relating some vital information about a patient, and then the patient dies because my powers prevented her from speaking?

CASSIE: If you had that kind of power, we'd be in business, now, wouldn't we?

GARY: What do you mean?

CASSIE: Oh, nothing. *(off of O.S. Nurse.)* Doesn't that bother you? That incessant talking?

GARY: Actually --

CASSIE: She's on depression medication because her father died five years ago. Five years ago! And on and on... That woman's like, what? Fifty? Yeah! I have a lot of faith in this place. I'll bet the nurses are all on meds, and the doctors are in the back fucking. Actually, this might work out nicely.

GARY: Maybe she needs them.

CASSIE: What? No. Addictions are for weak-minded people. Needs them! Grow up. Get a clue. Did the Jews have depression medication? No! They just fucking dealt with it.

GARY: Wow!

CASSIE: What? Are you Jewish?

GARY: No.

CASSIE: I mean, my father was a fucking bastard, but I dealt with it.

(He's speechless.)

CASSIE: I'm just joking. God! You're so serious! No, Daddy's great. He's on his way here to sit with the rest of us suckers and wait for the blessed event.

GARY: Is someone having a baby?

CASSIE: Aren't you cute? No. No births today.
    Only Death. Hopefully.

GARY: Wow!

CASSIE: I know, it's been like an hour and a half
    already. And you want to know why I've been
    tapping. What's your name?

GARY: Gary...

CASSIE: ... Okay. Not the curious type, I see.

(She tilts from side to side.)

CASSIE: God, my ass hurts! Does your ass hurt?

GARY: Yeah, a little. I guess.

CASSIE: Can you "will" us some cushions?

GARY: Defunct, I told you.

CASSIE: Right. Maybe that nurse can give me
    some pain pills, because the pain in my ass is
    unbearable.

(She gets up and stretches.)

GARY: *(re: Cassie's talking)* Mine too.

CASSIE: I mean, who the hell can sit in these?
    Well, I guess the majority of the 'Fat-Ass Na-
    tion' can. That should be our new name. Don't
    ya think? Not 'Land of the Free,' because that

doesn't quite cover it, but, 'Fat-Ass Nation.' It must be nice to walk around with your own personal built-in cushions --

GARY: Yeah, I could use some to cover my ears --

CASSIE: Me? I'd love it. I know, right? Who am I kidding? People would give their first-born child for my body. And probably their second, too. 'Cuz I've got a great ass. Don't you think? *(points to her butt)* Look. Here. In this area. Uh-huh!

(She licks her finger, sticks it on her butt and makes a sizzling sound. Then, she sits down abruptly and folds her hands demurely across her lap.)

CASSIE: Ladies don't talk like that, I know. They'd be so ruffled at the school. I get that a lot.

GARY: You get what a lot?

CASSIE: You want a soda? I'm out of caffeine. Not a good thing, believe me.

GARY: I'm good. Don't you think maybe you've had enough?

CASSIE: Oh, you mean my energy?

GARY: If that's what you call it.

CASSIE: I'm gathering up my energy. I have something to take care of soon.

GARY: For work, you mean? What do you do? Are you in school?

CASSIE: What? No. What do you do?

GARY: Games, huh?

CASSIE: Always. Do you want to get a game of Hangman or something going?

GARY: I don't think so.

CASSIE: Bad taste, right? I get that a lot...

GARY: ... Architect.

CASSIE: Whatever are you talking about? Who goes off on tangents like that?

GARY: I'm an architect. You asked what I do.

CASSIE: Oh... Oooo -- Do you "will" buildings up?

GARY: No, my powers haven't fully developed yet. And then, of course, there are times like these when I have to deal with short-circuit problems. No, I just design them.

CASSIE: Interesting. Sexy. I don't really have a boyfriend.

GARY: All part of the game, right?

(He looks at his watch.)

CASSIE: Don't look at your watch. It doesn't help. Believe me.

GARY: So, what does help?

CASSIE: Honestly?

GARY: No, let's skip to the end of our relationship and you can lie to me.

CASSIE: Ooo... We don't know each other well enough for that yet. And, I'm not a slut. Give it at least another twenty minutes.

GARY: For what? Now, I'm intrigued.

CASSIE: Now, you're intrigued. What were you before?

GARY: A little annoyed.

CASSIE: Why?

GARY: Because you were tapping.

CASSIE: Right! I forgot. Tapping is the crime of the century. You really have no idea about the crime I'm about to commit.

GARY: What? You're interrupting my train of thought again.

CASSIE: Sorry. What was I interrupting before?

GARY: I was making a list. In my head. A mental list.

CASSIE: This where I'm supposed to ask of what, right?

GARY: Since you ask, all sorts of things. I'm a list maker.

CASSIE: Interesting, and not at all sexy. What did this list consist of before I so rudely interrupted?

GARY: It was for my dog, Charlie, but then it morphed into a list about you.

CASSIE: Me? I'm so unbelievably honored! What was it about?

GARY: I didn't start my list right away. First, I tried to "will" you to shut up.

CASSIE: Oh.

GARY: Then, I summoned up all of my powers and gave you the "Death Stare."

CASSIE: What does it look like?

GARY: You saw it.

CASSIE: No, I didn't

GARY: This one.

(He stares at her.)

CASSIE: That's the "Death Stare?" I thought you were undressing me with your eyes!

GARY: No. You won't know when I'm doing that. That move is real slick. But after the "Death Stare" didn't work, I started my list: Number one -- Must kill the tapping girl. Then, you started to speak, and I thought, "Oh, she speaks. This is not good." Number two -- Must "will" ass cushions to muffle the sound of her voice.

CASSIE: Whatever that means.

GARY: Number three -- Must kill the boyfriend.

CASSIE: That's so sweet.

GARY: Number four -- Drinks too much caffeine. Watch that one. Number five -- Keep her away from all kitchen knives.

CASSIE: I'll ignore that one.

GARY: Number Six -- She's starting to look --

CASSIE: Wait. What was that last one? When would you and I ever be near kitchen knives together? Oh, you mean when we start our relationship and move in together? That's why you wanted to kill my mythical boyfriend! That is so sweet. I could kiss you. I'm almost ready to tell you what we could do to pass the time...

GARY: Number Six -- I'm composing now. She's starting to look real good to me. Take her for a walk to see my car in the parking --

CASSIE: Ooo... What kind of car?

GARY: What?

CASSIE: What kind of car does a list-making architect have?

GARY: No, the real question is, what kind of car would you like to sit in with me?

CASSIE: Okay. I'm getting horny now. I really am. And is that appropriate? I don't think so. Bad taste. You've caught my bad taste, do you know that? I love it.

GARY: Do you?

CASSIE: Yup...

(She looks O.S.)

GARY: What is it?

CASSIE: False alarm. I just thought I saw who it is I've been waiting for. I know it's silly, but I am absolutely convinced he's stuck in traffic.

GARY: Who?

CASSIE: ... Death.

GARY: What?

CASSIE: Death. The Grim Reaper? Let's get a soda. I'm thirsty. Want to?

GARY: Okay.

CASSIE: Just not diet. I hate diet. It's watered down crap!

SCENE 2: RUM AND COKE

(A few moments later. Cassie and Gary enter drinking sodas.)

CASSIE: So, I said, "I could have had a seat if you weren't so fat!" And then, I ran like hell!

GARY: But, she was nice enough to offer you a seat.

CASSIE: Were you listening to any part of the story? Her fat, actually pooled over into the next seat, and what she offered me was the hump of the seat. The ridge! I love a good time like the next girl, but I don't have to get my kicks on the ridge of a seat in a subway car like some people! I hate fat people! I really do. I don't mind giving up a little space every now and then, but when I'm being squished in my seat because someone didn't have enough control to put down the Cheetos, is that really my problem? Speaking of which, I am so going to miss spin today, aren't I?

GARY: What?

CASSIE: Spin class. For my ass?

GARY: You look like you could miss a class or two.

CASSIE: Ooo, flirting are we? And then fat people, like my grandmother, actually have the nerve to suggest that I'm anorexic! Anorexic! I guess they forget from their fat vantage point what a normal human body looks like. Minus the rolls of fat, caused by lack of self-control. I carry a picture of her around in my wallet. *(pulls photo out)* So, when she starts in with me. I just go, "Bam!" *(shoves picture in Gary's face)* See? My grandmother when she was eighteen. She forgot that she used to fit into a bikini. She was beautiful, wasn't she? Before she met my grandfather, and lost her whole life. Which is why I'm so damn gorgeous! I got my looks from him. The bastard.

GARY: Is that who's in there?

CASSIE: So, do you need another Coke? I'm buying. I know. I'm not supposed to use drinking language, like "I'm buying." At least, that's what they say at AA. But, seriously...

(She pulls out little alcohol bottles from her purse, and sits on the floor against the chairs.)

CASSIE: Let's have some rum and Coke!

GARY: Um.

CASSIE: Don't be a pussy.

GARY: No. It's not that.

CASSIE: So...?

GARY: Maybe we could take the rum and Coke to the car... If you want... Pass the time.

CASSIE: Oh, your car --

GARY: In the garage.

CASSIE: Of course...

GARY: Or, we could --

CASSIE: What?

GARY: Have some rum and Coke, and go later.

CASSIE: Okay.

GARY: I have some soda left. Want to share mine?

(She pours some rum in the can and they share.)

GARY: So, what's this about traffic? I was starting to think that freaky was looking good --

CASSIE: Freaky as in me.

GARY: Yeah, but now, I don't know, you just seem so angry.

CASSIE: It amazes me even that this tiny, svelte body can hold so much anger. I mean you're probably wondering, "What does she really have to be angry about? She's sexy, probably dynamite in bed --"

GARY: That's exactly what I was thinking --

CASSIE: I don't know. Education? No. Love life? Definitely a "no." Maybe, that I had to leave school and pay $15 for parking. Maybe family crap that never fucking ends! Well, if I'm lucky it will end today. Maybe the Grim Reaper could move his frigging ass and get here before visiting hours are up. Is that too much to ask? That you do your job?

GARY: Don't ask me. I just got fired.

CASSIE: You'd think I was at Starbucks having someone behind the counter ignore me as I order a latte. Hello! You have a death to attend to on the fourth floor ICU! Could you do your job? God! I would drag this chair into his room, and sit and watch forever for him to take his final bow. My ass would delight in that! And then, drinks for everybody! On me! They'd love that in AA. What are you thinking?

GARY: Honestly?

CASSIE: No. Remember, I enjoy lies. I live on them like diet pills.

GARY: I was thinking --

CASSIE: Yes --

GARY: I was wondering --

CASSIE: Speak to me.

GARY: What would happen to all of your energy if you weren't speaking. All of your anger.

CASSIE: You want me to stop talking? Okay, we're done here!

(She gets up to leave, but he pulls her back down.)

GARY: No, I was just thinking that if you didn't speak, you'd have no outlet for all of that energy. All of that violence.

CASSIE: Okay...

GARY: So, I was wondering if I could help relieve you of any of that pent-up energy...

CASSIE: Oh --

GARY: If you weren't talking.

CASSIE: I see.

GARY: Is there any way that I can help?

CASSIE: There's only one way you're thinking of.

GARY: Oh, no. There are multiple ways I'm thinking of.

CASSIE: Interesting.

GARY: I mean, you're going to miss step class and everything --

CASSIE: Spin.

GARY: What?

CASSIE: Spin class.

GARY: I thought that maybe you felt bad about not burning any calories. I'm thinking about you really.

(Death enters, crosses the stage and exits. Only Cassie sees Him.)

CASSIE: It's about time!

GARY: Oh, but I thought that we were talking --

CASSIE: No, not you -- I meant -- never mind.

(She moves to exit.)

GARY: Where are you -- ?

CASSIE: To see your car. Things look like they're about to be taken care of here. Do you want to show me, or what?

SCENE 3: AMAZON WOMEN

(An hour later, Cassie and Gary sit apart. Gary reads a magazine.)

CASSIE: I think I may be inherently pre-disposed to do something violent.

GARY: To me? I thought we had a good --

CASSIE: Not you, specifically. No.

GARY: Good.

(He continues reading.)

CASSIE: I just feel like I should have been raised by Amazon women, don't you?

GARY: What are -- ?

CASSIE: I think Amazon women eat their male young, actually, so that's not so good for you. But, it sounds great to me! Bare-breasted warriors, hanging all out. Snakes in their hair like Medusa. Women who know when it's time to help someone out of this world. I'll help him out of this world. Charge the hospital bed with my spear. Aim right for the face. Blood spurts everywhere! I would offer up his brains to the gods. I need to cleanse these women of his life. If I could make things clean and right, I would. If they don't put me in jail for too long. But, I think they would. The jury would regard him as a helpless old man. And, I'd get the chair. Uneducated, lower-class fucks! Pardon my French, but that's what you get with a so-called democracy. Do they have the death penalty here? If they cut off his morphine allotment, then there might be just a drop of justice in the world. I could live on a drop. Everyone says I eat like a bird anyway. I'm a hundred and two. Can you tell?

GARY: I thought I knocked all of the anger out of you. I think I made it worse! If you give me another couple of minutes, maybe we'll go to the garage again, and I could --

CASSIE: What? I'm not angry! I'm past anger. I am just deciding if I have to take care of somebody else's job.

GARY: Death, again?

CASSIE: Seriously, what the fuck is going on? I mean, how many deaths does this guy have to take care of in one day? If it was my job, I would be on top of it. You know, I say he, but I don't see why it can't be a she. Death should be a she. Isn't there anyone you'd like to kill?

GARY: Not at the moment, no.

CASSIE: Will you help me do it?

GARY: Do what? Are you insane?

CASSIE: Well, we know each other. Intimately now. In some cultures you would be considered my husband, so legally you'd have to take on all responsibility for my actions.

GARY: Which floor were crazies on again?

CASSIE: Chill out! Always so serious! Lighten up.

GARY: Sure. Okay. Tell me that part about offering up brains.

CASSIE: Which part?

GARY: I was just --

CASSIE: You don't take me seriously.

GARY: Oh no. I take you very seriously.

CASSIE: Where do you think they keep the knives around here?

GARY: I'm sure that you couldn't get near them if you tried. And, please don't try.

CASSIE: You don't think I could pull off "doctor?" I know. I don't have that healthy golf look about me. I could probably steal that uniform...

GARY: Scrubs?

CASSIE: That's it! And, if I could get near the knives, I could cut his balls off. Damn, a good butcher knife would be super handy.

GARY: They don't have butcher knives in hospi-
tals. Super?

CASSIE: A knife expert, are we?

GARY: Well, not really. I mean I do know about
kitchen knives.

CASSIE: You do?

GARY: Yeah... I like to cook.

CASSIE: Are you going to cook for me?

GARY: Now?

CASSIE: Friday or something. Unless you'd like
to cook up a seventy-nine-year-old man in the
hospital.

(No response.)

CASSIE: Bad taste. Right?

GARY: A little.

CASSIE: I get that a lot. Human flesh isn't very
tasty, anyway, I'm sure. I don't know! I don't!
You're looking at me like I would know. What
kind of animal do you think I am?

GARY: I already know what kind of animal you
are.

CASSIE: Why are you here? You didn't tell me.

GARY: You didn't ask.

CASSIE: I'm asking, ass!

GARY: Well, I'm not telling. You like to have secrets. I like to have secrets.

CASSIE: I don't have any secrets. My life is an open book. I'll tell anybody anything.

GARY: I've noticed.

CASSIE: What does that mean?

GARY: It means you're very open with people.

CASSIE: And that's a bad thing? Besides, I'm not open with people, actually. I hardly tell anybody anything. I'm a very private person. Reserved.

GARY: Classy.

CASSIE: What?

GARY: And nasty all at the same time.

CASSIE: I'll take that as a compliment.

GARY: Please do.

(He kisses her on the neck as Death enters.)

DEATH: *(to Cassie)* I need to speak with you, Little Goat.

28

(Gary hasn't noticed.)

CASSIE: I need another soda.

GARY: I'll get you one.

CASSIE: Okay. You get one, and I'll meet you at the car.

GARY: Diet, right?

CASSIE: What? No! It's watered --

GARY: Watered-down crap, I know.

(He exits.)

CASSIE: You wanted me?... Do you need my help?... Where the hell have you been! I've been waiting forever!

(Death turns to her.)

CASSIE: I mean --

DEATH: What is it you want?

CASSIE: You know --

DEATH: Exactly?

CASSIE: You know what I want.

DEATH: But, why?

CASSIE: You know why.

DEATH: He didn't hurt you. He hurt them.

CASSIE: But, that hurts me.

DEATH: That doesn't make any sense.

CASSIE: It doesn't have to make sense! You just have to do your fucking job, or I will!

(Cassie grabs his blade, but he puts his hand on her arm.)

DEATH: You will what? Exactly?

SCENE 4: LITTLE GOAT

(A half hour later in the hospital waiting room, Death sits next to Cassie. In a moment, Gary enters -- He can't see Death.)

GARY: *(to Cassie)* Where were you? I was waiting forever. I drank both sodas. Are you okay?

CASSIE: I had a meeting.

GARY: A meeting... Oh, with Death, you mean?

CASSIE: Yes. Do you have a problem with that? *(to Death)* Would you excuse us please?

GARY: Who are you...?

DEATH: *(to Cassie)* Okay, my Little Goat.

CASSIE: Stop calling me that!

(Death exits.)

GARY: Are you okay?

(Gary sits next to her and puts his arm around her.)

CASSIE: He won't stop calling me that! Goat! My Little Goat!

GARY: What?

CASSIE: I used to think I was the goat. The sacrifice.

GARY: I don't --

CASSIE: It's my fault!

GARY: I don't underst --

CASSIE: She wanted a relationship with him, and I was the offering! The virgin burned at the stake, or a goat with its neck cut open. I prefer to think of myself as a goat. I would like to be a goat that has horns, though. Do goats have horns? I would love to charge the hospital bed right now. Put my head down, scrape my hoof along the linoleum, and charge the bed in a heartbeat. His last heartbeat. I have to make things right. It's my responsibility. How can I just sit here and let things be?

GARY: Sometimes, we have to just let things be. Sometimes things just happen to us, and we go along. It feels like someone put us on a ride, and we just have to ride it out. You know? Sometimes we wish people were dead. I understand that. People get in our way. They attach themselves to us, feed on us. All of the sudden, out of nowhere, we become domesticated. Someone else decides what our life will be. I understand. I really do.

CASSIE: Who do you want to kill? I'll help you if you help me.

GARY: My Little Goat...

CASSIE: Don't call me that. I hate that.

GARY: No. It's cute. Just like you. Tough with horns, but cute, too.

CASSIE: Give me a new name.

GARY: What is your name?

CASSIE: Now you want to know? I'm not telling!

GARY: Come on. Now, I want to know. I want to know my Little Goat's name.

(He kisses her neck.)

CASSIE: Don't... Cassie.

GARY: Cassie?

CASSIE: Yup.

GARY: Oh...

CASSIE: Why? What the fuck?

GARY: I just thought you'd have a different name.

CASSIE: Like what? What do you -- ?

GARY: I don't know. Something stronger. Matilda. Cleopatra. Not something delicate like Cassie. But, I guess you are delicate...

CASSIE: I am not delicate. I'm fierce. And, I have to take care of something soon because asshole doesn't look like he can handle it!

GARY: I think you need to calm down.

CASSIE: I'm fine. What? Why do you feel trapped? What's running your life?

GARY: Right now? You. You are running my life. Right down to the parking garage!

(He picks her up and carries her off.)

SCENE 5: TRUTH

(A half hour later in the hospital waiting room, Cassie enters with Death close behind.)

CASSIE: Shut up!

DEATH: I've never heard of a slutty goat. They just don't exist in nature.

CASSIE: Shut the fuck up! Besides, this is not nature. This is a hospital!

DEATH: No, this is not nature, and you are not natural.

CASSIE: Natural? You want to talk about natural? How about that bastard in there --

DEATH: Which one? Your new Lover Boy or --

CASSIE: Who do you think I mean, asshole?

DEATH: Because I know something you don't know about Lover Boy.

CASSIE: And what would that be?

DEATH: Do you really want to know?

CASSIE: Besides, I already know everything I need to know about him. If you know what I mean!

DEATH: You think you know everything.

CASSIE: I know how I feel, and that's enough.

DEATH: You think feelings are reliable?

CASSIE: What else is there?

DEATH: Okay. You think feelings are reliable. Fine. Let's discuss feelings. Do you want to know what your mother feels right now?

CASSIE: Delusional.

DEATH: Not quite. And your grandmother?

CASSIE: Expectant. Just like me.

DEATH: Wrong again, Goat. And your brother, your father, your Lover Boy? Do you want truth or feelings?

CASSIE: Feelings are truth, asshole! And, I'm not in the mood for a philosophical discussion. Besides, are you permitted to talk about these things, or are you just supposed to show up, and do your fucking job?

DEATH: And how is your job going?

CASSIE: You were late today! Years late if you ask me, and if there was somebody that I could report you to, I would! I'm sure you wouldn't be fired, though. Because, there probably aren't a lot of people waiting in line to do your job. Well, actually, I would! In fact, I'll sign up! Where do I sign up?

DEATII: I thought we covered this.

CASSIE: What do you mean? Because of that blade thing?" You think I can't lift it.

DEATH: It's not just the blade thing.

CASSIE: There have to be a myriad of ways to kill people anyhow. Or do you have to only use pre-approved weapons. And, who approves them? I want to know, who's in charge of you?

DEATH: There is a skill involved, and a respect for life and death that you just don't have. As you so aptly demonstrated the first time we met.

CASSIE: A respect for death? You want me to have respect for death. You are Death, so in short, you want me to, what, have respect for you? It's all about ego, isn't it? I want something selfless, really. His death for their happiness.

DEATH: It will not give them happiness.

CASSIE: How do you know?

DEATH: They don't want his death. Not even your fat grandmother.

CASSIE: What do they want then, asshole? Enlighten me.

DEATH: Life. Love. Pictures of a happy family, even if it's a lie. It's their lie.

CASSIE: I'll bring them truth.

DEATH: You can't. You don't know the truth.

CASSIE: Then, fine, then, tell me the truth, then.

DEATH: Let's start with one right now.

(Gary enters with his head down.)

CASSIE: What's the matter?

GARY: I have to tell you something.

CASSIE: Okay…

GARY: You know I like you, right?

CASSIE: What the hell?

GARY: I have to go now.

CASSIE: Okay... So dinner, Friday?

GARY: I don't think so.

CASSIE: Are you going to call me?

GARY: I can't…

CASSIE: Are you going to tell me why?

GARY: I have --

CASSIE: Yes?

GARY: I was here waiting for...

CASSIE: Will you fucking talk?

GARY: My wife...

CASSIE: Of course.

GARY: And our baby. I just want you to know that I had a really great time, and if circumstances were different. The truth is that --

(Cassie slaps him.)

GARY: I never meant to hurt you. You just made me forget...

CASSIE: Be nice to Charlie, at least.

GARY: What?

CASSIE: Charlie! That's your dog, right? Or did you lie about that?

GARY: No. That's my dog. And, I didn't exactly lie. I just didn't tell the truth.

CASSIE: And, from where you sit, high on your perch, that is definitely not lying. Right?

GARY: I'm sorry.

CASSIE: Take care of Charlie, because you'd really be Super Dick if we added animal cruelty to your list of offenses.

GARY: I'll be nice. I am nice... To the dog.

(He exits.)

CASSIE: And, to them.

DEATH: Don't be mad at me. I didn't have sex with you in the parking garage while I had a wife and kid.

CASSIE: Twice.

DEATH: You're not my type.

CASSIE: I'm not anybody's type. He's just like... And, I'm just like --

DEATH: Yes.

CASSIE: Why is that?

DEATH: Do you want the truth?

CASSIE: No. Not really. I'm so fucking tired. Not just my body. My soul, you know? No. I guess you don't know, do you?... So, why were you late?

DEATH: I wasn't late. I was right on time. Just like the way you feel. It's how you should feel right now.

CASSIE: More philosophical crap! Don't talk to me about how I should feel. Why does he live so long? That's the main point.

DEATH: Well, actually --

CASSIE: What can life hold for him? He's the last one at the party, and we all want him to leave so we can clean up the mess. It's not worth my time. I'd rather hire a cleaning crew. You know, my brother would help me do it, if you won't --

DEATH: You're not listening --

CASSIE: And, if I paid that nurse in pain pills, she'd help me too! No, he should be there for Mom, when it's done. He's better suited for that. Comfort. She always preferred him. Mothers always do. He's a bastard sometimes, too. But, I love him, I guess.

DEATH: You need to stop --

CASSIE: I can get a card game going with that nurse. Not Hangman. I'm told that's bad taste. And, we can use pain pills as chips --

DEATH: You need to stop and breathe --

CASSIE: "I'll see your Prosac and I'll raise you two Valium." That Nurse Cratchit lady. She would have been best friends with the lady they called my "step-grandmother." Fucking junkie. Drank herself to death. Other families have secrets. Not ours. Right?

DEATH: Language.

CASSIE: I know. My real grandmother, the fat one, would flip if she heard me. "Ladies don't talk like that. Ladies cross their legs, and wear stockings." All the time? Even with open-toed shoes?

DEATH: She's old. A ladies' lady.

CASSIE: You know she clears her throat all the time? It used to annoy me really until I found out he collapsed a vocal cord or something. And I'm supposed to sit here and do nothing?

DEATH: I should tell you --

CASSIE: Do you know I've been imagining cancer as little Miss PacMans lately? Bright as day. In the middle of class. It gives me peace of mind to know that he's having trouble breathing. Pulling in the breath of life. I relish that! I'll have a hotdog with some extra relish, please! And put some mustard on it! You know? I can actually hear the video game music play? A cherry for the liver, a banana for the intestines! I've got to get a pink ribbon or something to wear. Ms. PacMan style. Bam-Bam style. Pink is definitely the new black. According to Vogue. Not that I have a subscription or anything. I'm not lame!

DEATH: There's more --

CASSIE: Stop.

DEATH: You need to--

CASSIE: No!

DEATH: Yes!

CASSIE: I already know!

DEATH: He's dead.

(Long beat.)

CASSIE: I know.

(She gets ill, and begins to heave.)

DEATH: So. Do you feel better?...

CASSIE: No.

DEATH: You have to let this go.

CASSIE: I can't. Who would I be without my anger?

DEATH: I see.

CASSIE: No, you don't. If I let it go, it's like I condone it. It's like I say, "It's okay that you hurt the people I love. That you hurt me."

DEATH: That's not what that means.

CASSIE: No?

DEATH: There is power in letting go.

CASSIE: There's power in anger.

DEATH: Do you feel powerful?

CASSIE: I feel tired. But, I feel like I have to be strong for them. They have no strength without me. I have to be the strong woman in the clan, you know?

DEATH: I know.

CASSIE: A warrior.

DEATH: Yes.

CASSIE: But, nobody recognizes my strength.

DEATH: That's because it isn't strength. It's just anger. Do you know what strength is? Your grandmother --

CASSIE: Stop --

DEATH: Strength is finding a way to find money --

CASSIE: Don't --

DEATH: Hiding your kids in the closet --

CASSIE: I can't! Shit!

DEATH: You can listen. That is strength. To look someone in the eyes, and try to see past the pain.

CASSIE: I can't. I can't be like them.

DEATH: Yes, you can. Your love makes you fierce.

CASSIE: I am, aren't I? Fierce, I mean?

DEATH: You already know.

CASSIE: But, I couldn't kill him.

DEATH: That's because you do have strength. How would you look your daughter in the eyes one day knowing that you've killed?

CASSIE: I didn't think about that.

DEATH: Yes, you did. I know you did. My Little Goat...

CASSIE: So, why were you late? Were you stuck in traffic?

DEATH: In a way. Yes. There was a kind of traffic. Yes.

CASSIE: So you don't think that I have "Grim Reaper" in my future.

DEATH: No.

CASSIE: Are you going to get in trouble?

DEATH: What do you mean?

CASSIE: Talking to me? Or is that part of the job description?

DEATH: No. I won't get in trouble. And it's not part of the job description.

CASSIE: *(flirting)* So, why did you take the time with me? Flirting with unemployment?

DEATH: I told you you're not my type.

CASSIE: So, what is your type?

DEATH: Honestly?

CASSIE: No. I can't handle any more today. But, I'm guessing "Bride of Frankenstein" type, right? Fingers falling off, musty smell? Am I on the right track? Or do you like animals? Goats maybe?

DEATH: You are relentless.

CASSIE: I am, aren't I? Shall I keep guessing?

DEATH: No, I have to go.

CASSIE: Oh. Will I see you again?

DEATH: You will.

CASSIE: Soon?

DEATH: Do you want to?

CASSIE: Well, not soon. Unless you want to visit some guy with me. His name is Gary, he drives a black Mercedes, leather interior, four door, nice, but he gets really upset when you spill soda inside. Oh, and he has a wife and a kid, and a dog named Charlie. Although, I don't know what kind of dog.

DEATH: I do.

CASSIE: Oh. Well, it was nice, don't misunderstand. But, not too soon okay?

DEATH: Okay.

(He kisses her on the forehead.)

CASSIE: That wasn't the "Kiss of Death!" Was it?

DEATH: No.

CASSIE: You are kinda cute. In a death-like way.

DEATH: Relentless! Bye, Goat.

(He exits.)

END OF PLAY.

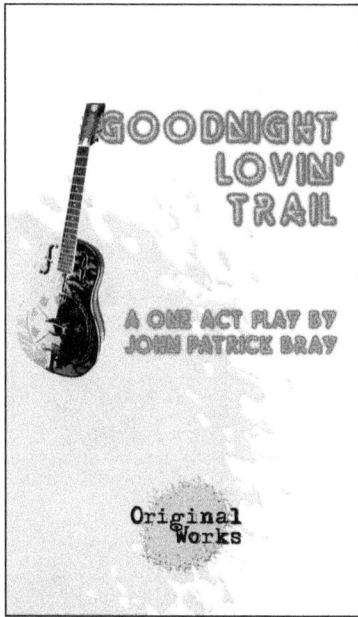

<u>Goodnight Lovin' Trail</u> by John Patrick Bray

Synopsis: This subtle and touching drama takes place at a truck stop diner in West Texas, where two desperate and lonely strangers find redemption in each other's eyes while discussing a stolen guitar. The play explores raw human emotions and consequences while these two desperate characters navigate and come to terms with the choices they've made on the road of life.

Cast Size: 1 Male, 1 Female

Mrs. Henderson's Cat by Lia Romeo

Synopsis: Cats do not have nine lives. And when 10-year-old dork Bobby and 11-year-old pageant princess Christine accidentally kill the cat they are supposed to be caring for, they go on the lam to avoid their inevitable punishment. In a plot that twists and turns like a kitty headed for the bathtub, grand theft auto, petty larceny, sugar highs, pop music, and hand holding run wild.

Cast Size: 1 Male, 1 Females

NOTES

NOTES

www.ingramcontent.com/pod-product-compliance
Lightning Source LLC
Chambersburg PA
CBHW071742020426
42331CB00008B/2142